LEARN TO PLAY C

TABLE

LEARN TO PLAY ON

TABLA

RAM AVTAR 'VIR'

Sangeet Acharya

PANKAJ

PUBLICATIONS

© RAM AVTAR 'VIR'

Revised Edition 1998

ISBN 81-87155-00-0

Published by
Pankaj Publications
M-114 Vikas Puri
New Delhi-110018

Sole Distributors :
Cambridge Book Depot
3. Regal Buildings
Sansad Marg,
New Delhi
Phone : 3363395
Fax : 91-11-5141173

Type setting at
Paragon Computers
B-36, Chanakya Place
New Delhi-110059
☎ 5509417

PANKAJ PUBLICATIONS

PREFACE

This book was originally printed in 1977. It received over-whelming response from the readers in general and the students of music, artists and art critics in particular which was beyond my expectations. The result was that the book printed in the first edition was sold out in a short time.

On the persistent demand of my pupils, friends, artists—professionals and amateurs,—land critics, I am bringing out this revised edition. It incorporates a few new features and suggestions I received from a few knowledgeable friends and well wishers. I have also taken this opportunity to deliminate errors of omission and commission which had crept in the first edition.

Indian Music is very much indebted to Amir Khusro who flourished during the reign of Allauddin Khilji in the 14th Century A.D. He was a poet, musician, musicologist and a statesman. He was also a devotee and Chief Lieutenant of Hazrat Nizam-u-din Aulia. In fact, he is recognized as the founder of Urdu Poetry. He made a rich contribution to the art of music and gave us two new musical instruments known as Sitar and Tabla.

Tabla has become very popular throughout India. No function—social or religious—is complete without it. Consequently, it has attracted the attention of a large number of students and lovers of music alike. In the absence of a reliable guide, it was difficult for them to learn the art of playing Tabla particularly so because of heavy cost involved in attending institutions imparting training in such arts or engaging experts for guiding at home. This book has, therefore, been brought out to meet the requirements of ever-increasing number of enthusiasts and lovers of art who can, with the help of a guide, learn it at home during their leisure hours.

1

I had originally written a number of books on the subject of musical instruments in Hindi. They adequately met the needs of Hindi Speaking population of India. To meet the requirements of Non-Hindi Speaking areas in the eastern and southern parts of our country as also of erstwhile Indians now settled in European, American and African countries, I have brought out English versions of these books. This book is one of those in the series.

This book deals with Tabla, its parts, nomenclature, boles, tuning as also with methods of its maintenance. It also covers methods of maintaining time and speed and general instructions for the guidance of beginners and amateurs. It also includes simple exercises with illustrations for their benefit. Some popular Thekas also form a useful part of this book.

This book has been published mainly for the guidance of beginners. Another book, "Tabla-2" has also been brought out which would be useful to advance students, amateurs and professionals alike. They are well advised to study that Part also which contains additional useful data and information like Mohra, Tukra, Paran, Tora and history of Tabla Gharanas.

I am sure this Revised Edition will be more useful and beneficial to my benevolent readers whose comments and suggestions for its improvement I shall be glad to receive for incorporation in the next revised edition.

Veeran Wali Bhawan,   **Ram Avtar 'Vir'**
M-24, Kirti Nagar,   Sangeet Acharya,
New Delhi-110 015.

CONTENTS

TABLA

Tabla is an important instrument in Indian Music. It is used widely with vocal and instrumental music as also with dancing. Ladies too have started learning the art of playing on Tabla. It makes the dance and music more attractive, melodious and enchanting.

Pakhavaj or Mridang is the mother of Tabla. Amir Khusro, a talented musician of the 14th Century A.D., split up Pakhavaj into two parts and developed a new musical instrument which he named Tabla after the name of an Arabian Instrument called Tabla. The right part was called Tabla and the left part was given the name of Duggi or Dhama.

Though Tabla was invented in the 14th Century A.D., it became popular only in the 18th Century after the Thumri Style of singing was introduced. Since then its popularity started gaining ground. By now, it has practically replaced Pakhavaj and Mridang in musical concerts.

PARTS OF TABLA, DHAMA AND DUGGI

1. Tabla(Right) — Khumbha (Wooden Drum)—It is made from a round block of sheesham wood, hollowed out from inside. It's top and bottom are round in shape. The circumference increase gradually from top to bottom.

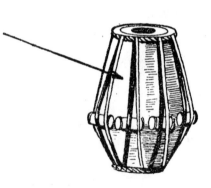

2. Dhama (Left)—Kumbha (Wooden Drum)—It is made from a round wooden block of mango or sheesham wood, hollowed out from inside. The circumference of top and bottom are nearly the same.

3. Duggi (Left)—A drum made of copper or brass nickelplated from outside. Circumference of its top is bigger than that of Tabla, Dhama.

4. Pudda (Top)—The tops of Tabla, Dhama and Duggi are made of skin of deer, fastened to the leather ring. The Puddas of Tabla and Duggi are pasted with black paste of iron filings in a circle having about 7cm dia.

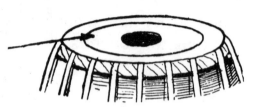

6

5. Deewal (Leather Brace)—A long leather brace is used for the purpose of holding the top of Tabla, Dhama or Duggi over the body of the drum.

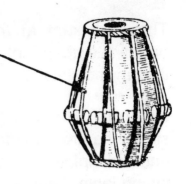

6. Gatta (Wooden Peg)—Gattas of 7cm × 3cm size and in cylindrical shape are used for tuning the Tabla. They are kept between the drum and the leather braces. They are made of mango or sheesham wood. Eight pegs are used in a Tabla.

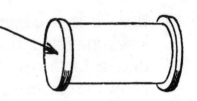

7. Langot (Leather Ring)—It is a small leather right which is kept at the bottom of Tabla, Dhama or Duggi for holding the leather braces joined together with the top of pudda stretched with leather braces.

8. Tekiyans (Seats)—Tekiyans are prepared from old rags in ring shape. Their circumference is about 30 cm. They are used for supporting Tabla, Dhama or Duggi to avoid movement.

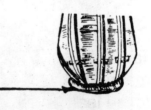

9. Gaddians (Top Cushions)—Top Cushions, circular in shape, are made of cloth and filled with cotton.

They are kept at the top of pudda (Leather Top) to protect it from moisture.

10. Hathorie (Hammer)—It is a simple hammer made of brass and nickelplated. It is used for tuning Tabla, Dhama and Duggi.

11. Box—It is a common wooden box large enough to accommodate a Table pair. It is used to keep the Tabla safe and free from dust, moisture and other destructive elements such as rats and insects.

SITTING POSITIONS

In the case of every musical instrument, the player has to take special care for sitting so that the may feel convenient in sounding the instrument as also in attracting the audience towards his art. In doing so, he has to take into consideration his style and position so that he may display his art in a beautiful manner. Taking these points into consideration, following sittings are recommended. The player may choose any of these according to his convenience and liking :

(A) Bending both the legs inside together and putting Tabla in front.

(B) Turning both the legs leftward and putting Tabla in front.

9

(C) Bending both the legs inside (as in A) together and putting the Duggi on the joint of legs and Tabla in front on the right side.

(D) Sitting as in C but placing the Duggi on the right leg and supported by the left leg. Tabla is placed in front of Duggi.

(E) Keeping the right leg upward and the left one horizontal to the ground—both in bent position—putting Tabla on the right touching the right leg and Duggi on the left touching the left knee.

Note :—The first three positions are commonly adopted by both males and females. The remaining two are generally used by male players.

BOLES (WORDS) ON TABLA

Just as points are fixed on any musical instrument to produce musical sound notes, similarly, points are fixed on the top of Tabla to produce sound of boles. The three points are Kinar (edge), Core (white portion)and Siyahi (black circle).

Tabla is divided into two parts i.e. Tabla and Duggi. Tabla is played by the right hand and Duggi by the left hand.

Boles on Tabla—There are six boles on Tabla which are produced by the right hand fingers. These six boles are Ta, Na, Tee, Tin, Te and Tay.

Ta or Na—This bole is produced on the edge of Tabla by a stroke of First Finger of the right hand.

Tee—This bole is produced on the white part between the edge and the black circle of top by a stroke of First Finger of the right hand.

Tin—This bole is produced on the black circle by the stroke of First Finger of the right hand.

The stroke should be very quick. The finger should be lifted as quickly as possible.

Te—Playing of this bole is a bit different from the three boles mentioned above. To produce it correctly, a combined stroke of Second, Third and Fourth Fingers is given on the black circle.

Tay—To produce this bole, a stroke of tip of the First Finger is given on the black circle. Keeping the other three Fingers in half standing position.

BOLES OF DUGGI

Only two boles namely Ge and Ke are produced on the top of Duggi. The boles Ge is also called Ghe white the bole Ke is also called Ka.

Ghe—The bole Ge (or Ghe) is produced by the left hand with the back portion of the palm resting on the white part of Duggi. The pressure of the arm should be light. The stroke should be given quickly by the tips in bent position of the First, Second and Third Fingers of the left hand on the black circle of the top. The fingers should not rest on the top.

Ke—This bole is produced by a joint stroke four fingers of the left hand on the black circle of the Duggi.

Joint boles on Tabla and Duggi— When boles of Tabla Ta, Duggi— When boles Ta, Na, Tee and Tin of Tabla are produced jointly with the boles Ghe of Duggi they are called Dha, Dhee and Dhin as follows :

Ta + Ghe = Dha,

Tee + Ghe = Dhee,

Tin + Ghe = Dhin

  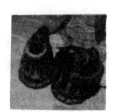

TAL AND LAY (TIME AND RHYTHM)

Talas—In Indian music element of time plays an important role. The regular succession of sound vibration is necessary to make sound musical. Also in vocal and instrumental music and dancing, intervals are created by clapping of hands. That is why it is called Tal.

Pakhavaj, Mridang, Dhol, Nakkara, Duff, Khanjari, Tabla etc., are the instruments used for the purpose of Talas. Out of these Tabla is the most popular instrument.

Ancient Indian musicians invented many Talas of different Matras (Strokes), Khand (Bars) and Boles (Words) and fixed the points of 'Sam', 'Talis' and 'Khalis' for every Tala.

Matra (Stroke)—A Matra is taken as the shortest time in which a syllable can be properly pronounced. In medium or normal speed, the time of a Matra is presumed to be one second, in fast speed it is half a second and in slow speed two seconds.

Boles—The sound produced by Tabla, Dhama or Duggi by the stroke of fingers and hand in different ways is called boles i.e. Ta, Na, Tee, Ke, Ge, Te, Tay, Dha, Dhee, Dhin.

Theka—The round of a Tala has fixed Matras and on every Matra there are fixed boles. They are called Thekas. For example, boles of Theka Tal Dadra (Matra 6) :

Sam				O	Khali	
Boles	Dhan	Dhin	Na	Dha	Tin	Na
Matras	1	2	3	4	5	6

Tali—Clapping of hand is called Tali i.e. Theka of Talas having Tali points marked 1, 2, 3, 4, etc.

Khali—Khali means a gap of some Matras which Boles of Theka play by right hand on Tabla only. The left (Duggi or Dhama) remains silent in Khali Matra's time.

13

Khali points help the classical musicians to understand the starting point of their Tala (Sam point) when they sing Khayal. Khali point on Theka, O sign on the Matra point is shown in every Tala.

Sam—The starting point of each Tala is called Sam. In other words, first Matra of Talas is Sam point and on every Theka it is shown by x sign.

Lay (Speed)—In ordinary sense, Lay means speed or any regular movements to complete a circle in a definite time. It is a natural, harmonious flow of vocal and instrumental sound and also a regular succession of accent. There are three types of speed in Indian music. All Percussion Instruments are used to control and regularize the musical sound.

The Three Types of Lay are :
A—Madhya Lay (Medium or Normal speed).
B—Drut Lay (Quick or Fast speed).
C—Vilambit Lay (Slow speed).

Madhya Lay (Medium or Normal Speed)—It is the time required by musicians to complete a round or a circle of a part of song, tune or dance in an easy way without exertion. Normal speed is the base of the remaining two speeds i.e., fast speed and slow speed.

Drut Lay (Quick or Fast Speed)—Fast speed means half the time of normal speed i.e., if a musician requires one minute time to complete a part of a song, tune or dance, in normal speed he will require half a minute to complete that part in Fast Speed.

Slow Speed—In slow speed a musician takes double the time to complete the round required by the medium or normal speed. If he completes a round of his play in one minute in normal speed, he will take two minutes to complete the same round in Slow Speed.

TUNING OF TABLA

It is very essential for every Tabla player to be very well conversant with the exact tuning of Tabla. An un-tuned Tabla always confuses the player. He is then unable to produce harmony and cannot attract the audience.

Types of Tabla Tuning

There are three types of Tabla Tuning. They are based on :—
1. Natural sound of drum.
2. Musician's basic note i.e. Shadaj (Sa) (C).
3. Harmonic Notes such as Madhyam (Ma) (F) or Pancham (Pa) (G) of Musician's Basic Notes (Sa) (C). This type of tuning is called Shadaj Madhyam (Sa-Ma) and Shadaj Pancham (Sa-Pa).

The learner should take the help of Harmonium for Tabla Tuning. It is an easy way for him to pick up the sound of the note to tune his Tabla, because the sound of Tabla should be tuned according to the sound of the Harmonium note.

Tuning of Tabla Based on Natural Sound of Drum—Every Tabla Drum, according to its size, gives natural sound when given a stroke by fingers on the Top (Pudda). The sound of Tabla depends upon two things :—

(a) Height of Tabla and (b) Circumference of its top.

The Tabla having wider circumference of top and greater height produces lower pitch. On the other hand, Tabla having comparatively smaller top circumference and lesser height produces higher pitch.

Tuning of Tabla Based on Musician's Basic Note i.e. Shadaj (Sa) (C) or Madhyam (Ma) (F) or Pancham (Pa) (G)—The Tabla (Right) should be tuned on the musician's fixed note for this purpose. One can take help of Harmonium, Piano and Organ. The voice of Note (Swar) which is used for Tabla Tuning, should be kept in mind before the start of Tabla Tuning because the sound of fixed note should be produced on Tabla on every point around it equally.

Method of Tuning

For Tuning of Tabla; a small hammer may be used. Before using the hammer, the top of Tabla should be tightened with the bottom small ring by leather braces. The pegs should be placed between the drum and leather braces. Four braces should be kept over every peg. In all eight pegs are used in a Tabla.

Use of Hammer

For the adjustment of upto 3 notes, the stroke of hammer used on pegs. When a stroke is given from top downwards, the sound should be raised and when the stroke is given from bottom upwards the sound should fall down.

Half note difference can be adjusted on top by hammer stroke given on the top ring hole points.

Tuning Points

When starting Tuning of Tabla and using the hammer on top, strike the top with right hand first finger and give a hammer stroke with left hand and hear the sound produced. Tally it with the sound of note fixed for the tuning produced by harmonium or by any other musical instrument.

If the sound is lower than that of the fixed note, then give a hammer stroke from top downward and if the sound is higher than that of the tuning note then give a hammer stroke from bottom upwards and check the sound by the right hand first finger gradually.

Note : Some musicians use right hand for hammer and left hand first finger for adjustment of tune.

In the system of Top tuning shown in Fig. No. A, Point Numbers are as follows :—

First Point is on hole No. 1
Second Point is on hole No. 9 opposite to hole No. 1
Third Point is on hole No. 5
Fourth Point is on hole No. 13 opposite to hole No. 5

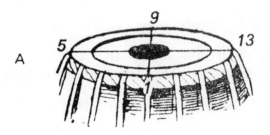

When these four points are tuned, then start further upper ring for tuning of remaining portions according to the given hole numbers as follows :—

(16-2), (15-3), (8-10), (7-11), (4-6), and (12-14).

When the whole circle is tuned, the top sound can be checked by the combined loose stroke (chanti) of Fingers No. 2, 3 & 4 of right hand.

Tuning of Dhama or Duggi :—For the tuning of Dhama or Duggi only two note sounds are used. The sound of note of Tabla is the base. According to that sound, first system is Shadaj (Sa) of Mandra Saptak (C of lower octave) and second is Pancham (Pa) of Mandra Saptak (G of lower octave). Both the systems are used according to the choice of the players and the size of Duggis.

SUGGESTIONS TO THE BEGINNERS

Tabla is not as melodious and interesting as other instruments are. Hence, a player may become a bit disinterested in the beginning. So it requires a patience of mind. The beginner should bear the following points in mind :—

(1) He should always play on the Tuned Tabla.

(2) The points on the top of Tabla and Duggi to produce boles should be remembered very carefully.

(3) It is very essential to maintain the speed of playing Theka.

(4) At the time of playing on Tabla the boles should be very clear and correct.

(5) The knowledge and the practice of hands is necessary for Tali and Khali points.

(6) The Sam points (Boles) should be very clear and distinctive from other boles.

(7) When playing on Tabla in the company of musicians, the Sam point of Tune or song must be recognized and the start of Theka should be made from the same Sam point. The player should adjust his speed with that of musician's speed.

(8) At the time of playing on Tabla, the player should be very careful about his facial expression and the presentation on Art.

(9) For every beginner, it is essential to remember boles of every Theka by heart and at the time of practice every bole should be spoken from the mouth.

(10) He should make a regular practice of one hour minimum daily.

MAINTENANCE OF TABLA

Tabla is a precious percussion instrument. Its top is generally destroyed by seasonal moisture, worms and rats. The following points should be kept in mind to maintain it properly :—

1. In hot season the Tabla should not be kept in a box in upper note Tuned position. Make it one or two notes down because a high pitch tuned top of Tabla may burst out due to heat.

2. The top of Tabla should be protected from the atmospheric moisture. A moist-topped Tabla should not be used for playing unless its moisture is removed either by solar heat or by fire. After using Tabla, cover the top with a cotton cushion.

3. The top of Tabla should be kept clean to produce correct sound. Clean it with petrol and dry it in the sun. When the leather braces become dry and hard, apply oil to make them soft.

RIGHT HAND EXERCISE

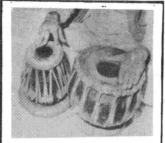

Ta   Na   Ta   Na   Ta   Na   Ta   Na
Ta   Na   Ta   Na   Ta   Na   Ta   Na

Tee Tee Tee Tee Tee Tee Tee Tee
Tee Tee Tee Tee Tee Tee Tee Tee

Tin Tin Tin Tin Tin Tin Tin Tin
Tin Tin Tin Tin Tin Tin Tin Tin

Ta Tee Tin Ta Tee Tin Ta Tee Tin
Ta Tee Tin Ta Tee Tin Ta Tee Tin

Te Na Te Na Te Na Te Na
Te Na Te Na Te Na Te Na

LEFT HAND EXERCISE

Ke   Ke   Ke   Ke   Ke   Ke   Ke   Ke
Ke   Ke   Ke   Ke   Ke   Ke   Ke   Ke

Ge   Ghe Ge   Ghe Ge   Ghe Ge   Ghe
Ge   Ghe Ge   Ghe Ge   Ghe Ge   Ghe

BOTH HANDS EXERCISE

Ta+Ghe=Dha—Tee+Ghe=Dhee
Tin+Ghe=Dhin

Dha Dhee Dhin Dha Dhee Dhin
Dha Dhee Dhin Dha Dhee Dhin

TAL KEHRWA

Matras (Beats)	4
Khand (Bar)	1 of four Beats
Sam	On first Beat
Tali	On first Beat

BOLES OF THEKA TAL KEHRWA

Sam			
X			
1	2	3	4
Dhin	Dha	Tin	Na

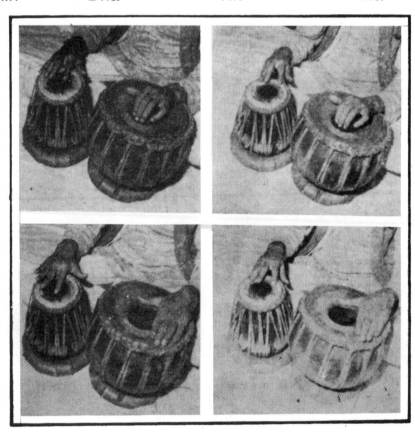

TAL KEHRWA

Matras (Beats)	8
Khand (Bars)	2, 4 Beats in each Bar
Sam x	On first Beat
Tali	On first Beat
Dhali	On fifth Beat

BOLES OF THEKA TAL KEHRWA

Sam				Khali			
x				0			
1	2	3	4	5	6	7	8
Dha	Ge	Na	Tee	Ta	Ke	Dhin	Ne

TAL DADRA

Matras (Beats)	6
Khand (Bars)	Two Bars having 3 Beats in each
Sam x	On first Beat
Talis=1	On first,
Khali 0	On fourth Beat

BOLES OF THEKA TAL DADRA

Sam			Khali		
x			0		
1	2	3	4	5	6
Dha	Dhin	Na	Dha	Tin	Na

TAL JHAPA

Matras (Beats)	10
Khand (Bars)	4 two Bars having 2 Beats in each and Two Bars having 3 Beats in each
Sam x	On first Beat
Talis=3	On First, Third & Eighth Beat
Khali 0	On Sixth Beat

BOLES OF THEKA TAL JHAPA

Sam x		Tali 2			Khali 0		Tali 3		
1	2	3	4	5	6	7	8	9	10
Dhin	Na	Dhin	Dhin	Na	Tin	Na	Dhin	Dhin	Na

 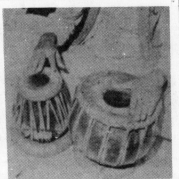

25

BOLES OF THEKA TAL JHAPA

Sam		Tali			Khali		Tali		
x		2			0		3		
1	2	3	4	5	6	7	8	9	10
Dhin	Na	Dhin	Dhin	Na	Tin	Na	Dhin	Dhin	Na

Boles of Theka Tal Jhapa (Type-2)

Sam		Tali			Khali		Tali		
x		2			0		3		
1	2	3	4	5	6	7	8	9	10
Dhin	Nak	Dhin	Dhin	Nak	Tin	Nak	Dhin	Dhin	Nak

TAL EK TAL

Matras (Beats)	**12**
Khand (Bars)	**6 (2 Beats in each Bar)**
Sam x	**On first Beat**
Talis, 4	**On first, fifth, ninth & eleventh**
Khali On 0 = 2	**On third & seventh**

BOLES OF THEKA TAL EK TAL

Sam		Khali		Tali		Khali		Tali		Tali	
x		0		2		0		3		4	
1	2	3	4	5	6	7	8	9	10	11	12
Dhin	Dhin	Dhage	Tirkit	Too	Na	Kat	Ta	Dhage	Tirkit	Dhin	Na

TAL TEEN

Matras (Beats)   16
Khand (Bars)   4 (4 Beats in each Bar)
Sam x   On 1st Beat
Talis 3   On 1st, fifth & thirteenth Beat
Khali 0=1   Ninth Beat

BOLES OF THEKA TAL TEEN

Sam X				Tali 2				Khali 0				Tali 3			
1	2	3	4	5	6	7	8	9	10	11	12	13	14	15	16
Dha	Dhin	Dhin	Dha	Dha	Dhin	Dhin	Dha	Dha	Tin	Tin	Ta	Ta	Dhin	Dhin	Dha

BOLES OF THEKA TAL TEEN

Sam X				Tali 2				Khali 0				Tali 3			
1	2	3	4	5	6	7	8	9	10	11	12	13	14	15	16
Dha	Dhin	Dhin	Dha	Dha	Dhin	Dhin	Dha	Dha	Tin	Tin	Ta	Ta	Dhin	Dhin	Dha

BOLES OF THEKA TAL TEEN (TYPE-2)

Sam X				Tali 2				Khali 0				Tali 3			
1	2	3	4	5	6	7	8	9	10	11	12	13	14	15	16
Na	Dhi	Dhi	Na	Na	Dhi	Dhi	Na	Na	Tee	Tee	Na	Na	Dhi	Dhi	Na

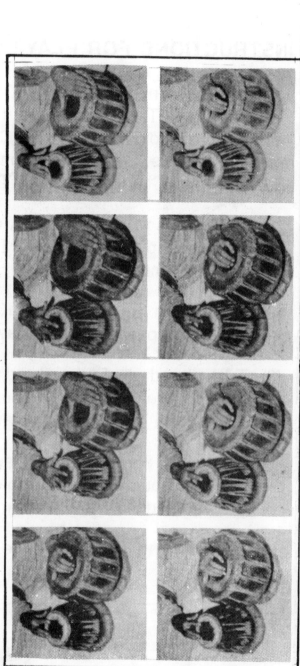

29

INSTRUCTIONS FOR PLAYING ADVANCE TALAS

You have by now practised Tal Dadra, Tal Kehrwa, Jhaap Tal, Ek Tal and Teen Tal. We are now giving below details with illustrations of Talwara and Ara Chautal, which are played with big Khayals. On the occasions of festivals like Hori, Dhamar, Deep Chandi and Rupak Tal, 7 Matras are played.

(1) All the Talas you have learnt by now should be practised regularly and daily by repeating the strokes twice, thrice and four times.

(2) Talas which are played with Khayal should be played with slow speed (Vilambat Lay).

(3) Talas played with Dhrupad and Dhamar should be practised with free boles i.e., by four fingers of hands joined together on Tabla and Dhama or Duggi.

Exercises in playing of Dadra and Kehrwa Talas in double, treble and four times are being given. Similarly, exercise for Teen Tal — double and four times is given.

The remaining Talas should be practised accordingly.

EXERCISE TAL DADRA

X		O		
Dha	Dhin	Na	Dha	Tin	Na

DOUBLE

X   O

Dha Dhin   Na Dha Tin Na | Dha Dhin   Na Dha Tin Na

TREBLE

X

Dha Dhin Na   Dha Tin Na   Dha Dhin Na

O

Dha Tin Na   Dha Dhin Na   Dha Tin Na

FOUR TIMES

X   O

Dha   Dhin   Na   Dha   Tin   Na   Dha   Dhin

Na   Dha   Tin   Na   Dha   Dhin   Na   Dha

Tin   Na   Dha   Dhin   Na   Dham   Tin   Na

EXERCISE TAL KEHRWA

X				O			
Dha	Ge	Na	Ti	Na	Ke	Dhin	Na

DOUBLE

X

Dha Ge   Na ti   Ta Ke   Dhin Na

O

Dha Ge   Na ti   Ta Ke   Dhin Na

TREBLE

X

Dha Ge Na   Ti Na Ke   Dhin Na Dha

Ge Na Ti   Na Ke Dhin   Na Dha Ge

O

Na Ti Na   Ke Dhin Na   Dha Ge Na

X

Ti Na Ke   Dhin Na Dha   Ge Na Ti

O

Na Ke Dhin   Na Dha Ge   Ti Na Ka

FOUR TIMES

X							
Dha	Ge	Na	Ti	Ta	Ke	Dhin	Na
Dha	Ge	Na	Ti	Ta	Ke	Dhin	Na
Dha	Ge	Na	Ti	Ta	Ke	Dhin	Na
Dha	Ge	Na	Ti	Ta	Ke	Dhin	Na

BOLES OF THEKA TAL TEEN

Sam				Tali				Khali				Tali			
X				2				O				3			
1	2	3	4	5	6	7	8	9	10	11	12	13	14	15	16
Dha	Dhin	Dhin	Dha	Dha	Dhin	Dhin	Dha	Dha	Tin	Tin	Ta	Ta	Dhin	Dhin	Dha

DOUBLE

X															
Dha	Dhin	Dhin	Dha	Dha	Dhin	Dhin	Dha	Dha	Tin	Tin	Ta	Ta	Dhin	Dhin	Dha
2															
Dha	Dhin	Dhin	Dha	Dha	Dhin	Dhin	Dha	Dha	Tin	Tin	Ta	Ta	Dhin	Dhin	Dha
3															
O															

FOUR TIMES

Dha	Dhin	Dhin	Dha	Dha	Dhin	Dhin	Dha	Dha	Tin	Tin	Ta	Ta	Dhin	Dhin	Dha
Dha	Tin	Tin	Ta	Ta	Dhin	Dhin	Dha	Dha	Dhin	Dhin	Dha	Dha	Dhin	Dhin	Dha
2															
Dha	Dhin	Dhin	Dha	Dha	Dhin	Dhin	Dha	Dha	Tin	Tin	Ta	Ta	Dhin	Dhin	Dha
Dha	Tin	Tin	Ta	Ta	Dhin	Dhin	Dha	Dha	Dhin	Dhin	Dha	Dha	Dhin	Dhin	Dha
O															
Dha	Dhin	Dhin	Dha	Dha	Dhin	Dhin	Dha	Dha	Tin	Tin	Ta	Ta	Dhin	Dhin	Dha
Dha	Tin	Tin	Ta	Ta	Dhin	Dhin	Dha	Dha	Dhin	Dhin	Dha	Dha	Dhin	Dhin	Dha
3															
Dha	Dhin	Dhin	Dha	Dha	Dhin	Dhin	Dha	Dha	Tin	Tin	Ta	Ta	Dhin	Dhin	Dha
Dha	Tin	Tin	Ta	Ta	Dhin	Dhin	Dha	Dha	Dhin	Dhin	Dha	Dha	Dhin	Dhin	Dha

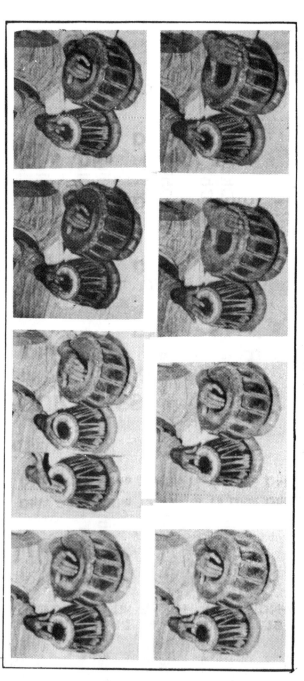

TAL TALWARA MATRA 16

This Theka is played with Bara Khiyal. It contains 16 matras—4 bars of 4 matras each. Sam point is on first matra and Tali on 1, 5 and 13th matra and Khali on 9th matra.

BOLES OF THEKA TAL TALWARA, MATRA 16

Sam X				Tali 2				Khali 0				Tali 3			
1	2	3	4	5	6	7	8	9	10	11	12	13	14	15	16
Dha	Trik	Dhin	Dhin	Dha	Dha	Tin	Tin	Ta	Trik	Dhin	Dhin	Dha	Dha	Dhin	Dhi

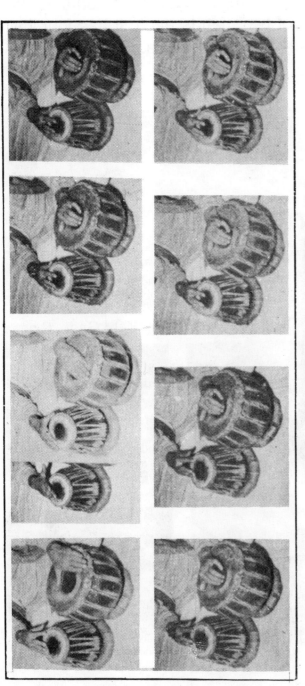

TAL TALWARA MATRA 16

This Theka is played with Bara Khiyal. It contains 16 matras—4 bars of 4 matras each. Sam point is on first matra and Tali on 1, 5 and 13th matra and Khali on 9th matra.

BOLES OF THEKA TAL TALWARA, MATRA 16

Sam X				Tali 2				Khali 0				Tali 3			
1	2	3	4	5	6	7	8	9	10	11	12	13	14	15	16
Dha	Trik	Dhin	Dhin	Dha	Dha	Tin	Tin	Ta	Trik	Dhin	Dhin	Dha	Dha	Dhin	Dhi

THEKA TAL CHAR, MATRA 12

This Theka is played with Dhrupad Gayan. It contains 12 matras divided into six bars of two matras each. It has four Tali and two Khali points. Its sam is on first matra.

BOLES OF THEKA CHAR TAL

X		0		2		0		3		4	
1	2	3	4	5	6	7	8	9	10	11	12
Dha	Dha	Din	Ta	Kit	Dha	Din	Ta	Tit	Kat	Gadi	Gina

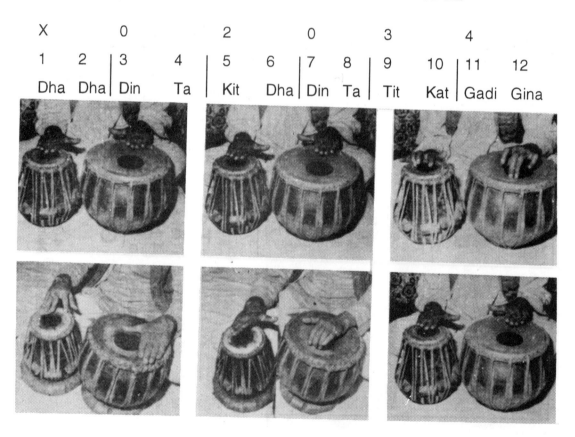

THEKA TAL CHAR, MATRA 12

This Theka is played with Dhrupad Gayan. It contains 12 matras divided into six bars of two matras each. It has four Tali and two Khali points. Its sam is on first matra.

BOLES OF THEKA CHAR TAL

X		0		2		0		3		4	
1	2	3	4	5	6	7	8	9	10	11	12
Dha	Dha	Din	Ta	Kit	Dha	Din	Ta	Tit	Kat	Gadi	Gina

TAL ARA CHAUTAL, MATRA 14

This Theka is played with Dhrupad Gayam. It contains 14 matras in 7 bars of 2 matras each. Its sam is on first matra. It contains 4 tali and 3 khali points. Tali on first, third, 7th and eleventh points and Khali on fifth, ninth and thirteenth point.

BOLES OF THEKA TAL ARA CHAUTAL

X		2		0		3		0		4		0	
1	2	3	4	5	6	7	8	9	10	11	12	13	14
Dhin	Trik	Dhin	Na	Too	Na	Ka	Ta	Trik	Dhin	Na	Dhin	Dhin	Na

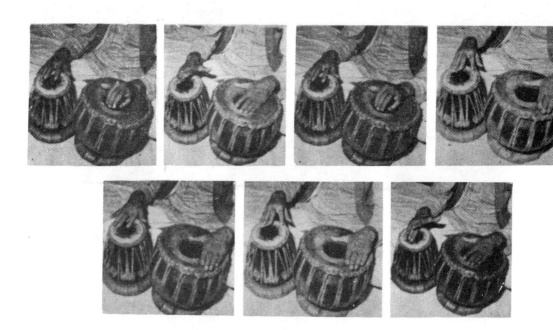

TAL ARA CHAUTAL, MATRA 14

This Theka is played with Dhrupad Gayam. It contains 14 matras in 7 bars of 2 matras each. Its sam is on first matra. It contains 4 tali and 3 khali points. Tali on first, third, 7th and eleventh points and Khali on fifth, ninth and thirteenth point.

BOLES OF THEKA TAL ARA CHAUTAL

X		2		0		3		0		4		0	
1	2	3	4	5	6	7	8	9	10	11	12	13	14
Dhin	Trik	Dhin	Na	Too	Na	Ka	Ta	Trik	Dhin	Na	Dhin	Dhin	Na

39

THEKA TAL DEEP CHANDI MATRA 14

It contains 14 matras in 4 bars—two bars of three matras and two of four matras each.

Its sam point is on first matra, Tali point of first, fourth and eleventh and Khali point on eighth matra.

THEKA TAL DEEP CHANDI MATRA 14

1			2				0			2			
1	2	3	4	5	6	7	8	9	10	11	12	13	14
Dha	Dhin	—	Dha	Ge	Tin	—	Ta	Tin	—	Dha	Ge	Tin	—

THEKA TAL DEEP CHANDI MATRA 14

It contains 14 matras in 4 bars—two bars of three matras and two of four matras each.

Its sam point is on first matra, Tali point of first, fourth and eleventh and Khali point on eighth matra.

THEKA TAL DEEP CHANDI MATRA 14

1			2				0			2			
1	2	3	4	5	6	7	8	9	10	11	12	13	14
Dha	Dhin	—	Dha	Ge	Tin	—	Ta	Tin	—	Dha	Ge	Tin	—

TAL DHAMAR MATRA 14

It contains 14 matras in four bars—first bar of 5 matras, second bar of two matras, third of 3 matras and fourth of 4 matras.

Its sam point is on first matra. Its Tali Points are on first, sixth and eleventh matra and Khali point on eighth matra.

BOLES OF THEKA TAL DHAMAR

X			2				0			3			
1	2	3	4	5	6	7	8	9	10	11	12	13	14
Ka	Dhi	Ta	Dhi	Ta	Dha	—	Ge	Te	Ta	Te	Ta	Ta	—

TAL DHAMAR MATRA 14

It contains 14 matras in four bars—first bar of 5 matras, second bar of two matras, third of 3 matras and fourth of 4 matras.

Its sam point is on first matra. Its Tali Points are on first, sixth and eleventh matra and Khali point on eighth matra.

BOLES OF THEKA TAL DHAMAR

X				2		0			3			
1	2	3	4	5	6	7	8	9	10	11	12	13	14
Ka	Dhi	Ta	Dhi	Ta	Dha	—	Ge	Te	Ta	Te	Ta	Ta	—

43

TAL TEEVRA MATRA 7

It contains seven matras in three bars—two bars of two matras each and one bar of three matras. Sam point is on first matra, Tali on first, fourth and sixth points. There is no Khali point in this Tal. It is generally played with Bhajans, Geets and Ghazals.

BOLES OF THEKA TAL TEEVRA MATRA 7

Sam			Tali		Tali	
1			2		3	
1	2	3	4	5	6	7
Dha	Dhi	Ta	Tite	Kat	Gadi	Gin

THEKA TAL ROOPAK, MATRA 7

It contains seven matras in three bars—two bars of two matras each and one bar of three matras. Sam point is on first matra, Tali on first, fourth and sixth points. There is no Khali point in this Tal. It is generally played with Bhajans, Geets and Ghazals.

BOLES OF THEKA TAL TEEVRA MATRA 7

0			2		3	
1	2	3	4	5	6	7
Tin	Tin	Na	Dhin	Na	Dhin	Na

SOME IMPORTANT EXERCISES

1. Na   Tin   Ge   Dha   Ke   Ta   Dha   Dhin

DOUBLE

Na Na   Tin Tin   Ge Ge   Dha Dha   Ke Ke

Ta Ta   Dha Dha   Dhin Dhin

TREBLE

Na Na Na   Tin Tin Tin   Ge Ge Ge   Dha Dha Dha

Ke Ke Ke   Ta Ta Ta   Dha Dha Dha   Dhin Dhin Dhin

FOUR TIMES

Na Na Na Na   Tin Tin Tin Tin   Ge Ge Ge Ge

Dha Dha Dha Dha   Ke Ke Ke Ke   Ta Ta Ta Ta

Dha Dha Dha Dha   Dhin Dhin Dhin Dhin

2.   Ta Ta   Ta Ge   Dha Dha

      Dha Ge   Na Ta   Ta Ge

      Dha Dha   Dha Ge

IMPORTANT EXERCISES FOR LEFT HAND

1.   Ge Ge   Dha Dha   Ke Ke   Ta Ta

2.   Ge Ge   Ge Dha   Ke Ke   Ke Ta

3.   Ge Ge   Ge Ge   Dha Ge   Dha Ge

4.   Dha Ge   Ge Ge   Ge Ge   Dha Dha

5.   Dha Ge   Dha Ge   Ge Ge   Dha Ge
        Ta Ke   Ta Ke   Ge Ge   Dha Ge

6.   Dha Ge   Ge Dha   Ge Ge   Dha —
        Ta Ke   Ke Ta   Ge Ge   Dha —

7.   Ge Ge   Ge Dha   — Ge   Ge Ge
        Ge —   Ge Ge   — Dha   Ge Ge

8.   Ge Ge   Dha Ge   Dha Ge   Ge Ge
        Ge Ge   Ta Ge   Dha Ge   Ge Ge